Music Minus One Trumpet
Also suitable for any B♭ Instrument

THE FINE ART OF
BALLAD PLAYING

Standards for Trumpet, Vol. 6

MMO
6846

This collection of songs is derived from the classic recording of 1956 by Frank Sinatra with the orchestrations of master arranger Nelson Riddle.

When Irv Kratka, the founder of Music Minus One asked me to do a trumpet version of the Sinatra/Riddle collaboration I got very excited because back in 1956 while stationed at Bolling Air Force base in Washington, DC with the Airmen Of Note, the USAF Glenn Miller Band, I literally wore out that 33 1/3 rpm LP record! *(If you remember those long-playing discs you're either a senior like me or an audiophile extraordinaire.)* And here am I more than a half a century later having recorded my renditions with the very same, unique background tracks!

So here goes with the notes and comments on this my sixth album in the series of standards for Trumpet, Flugel Horn and other Bb instruments.

Perhaps a "disclaimer" is necessary to explain how I instructed my transcriber to approach the notating of my solos. They are purposely not 100% literal transcriptions in order for the notation not to be overwhelmingly complex. Rather I wanted them to be "user-friendly," so with that said, I suggest you listen carefully for the subtleties in rhythmic nuances especially. A major part of your training is to recognize these nuances in order to add them to your "tool box" for ballad styling.

And that brings me to the title of this volume, **The Fine Art Of Ballad Playing.** Those of you who have had formal trumpet education will recall that an essential part of the Arban Book is **The Art Of Phrasing** which with its 150 Classic and Popular Melodies had a similar purpose to my series of standards. Perhaps if Professor Arban had the technology available to him, he would have included a CD of his renditions of those melodies for students to emulate. Although those melodies are obviously not from the Great American Song Book, the concepts of expression, dynamics and phrasing remain all important.

In all of these renditions, I chose to be "faithful to Frank" who had a unique way of rarely straying far from the actual melody, especially on ballads, while always putting his "Sinatra Stamp" on it! Very simply put, think lyrics and "story" and that will guide you through the flow of the melody with it's "peaks and valleys". If you've not done this kind of study or training before, please realize it's totally okay to imitate and that's where the great value of Music Minus One comes in.

In a way, with this sixth volume in the series we're returning to the essential skill to acquire and that is, know and play the actual melody and learn how through listening and imitation to make the most of that existing melody rather than trying to invent a new one. Remember that seventh step in my Natural or Ear-based Approach to Acquiring Jazz styling and Improvisational Skills? There's a time for that step and perhaps I will demonstrate the creating of new melodies on the existing chord structure of these songs at a later time on a video tutorial.

By the way, if you click on these links you can view two videos on YouTube that I made for Music Minus One which elucidate my seven step program.

http://www.youtube.com/watch?v=FMjlrvk1gnE

http://www.youtube.com/watch?v=f-wHib9iZ8U

Also, it can be very advantageous to listen to the original Sinatra/Riddle recording. All of these songs can be heard on YouTube. This Sinatra fan has posted them at:

http://www.youtube.com/user/SinatraFan64/videos

With the title song In **The Wee Small Hours Of The Morning** the overall mood of the album is set of sadness, unrequited love and loneliness. With this unusually short song that message is poignantly delivered and while you don't have lyrics actually coming out of your horn to express the emotions, if you know and keep them in mind while playing, the feelings will be sure to come through!

I'll Be Around is a beautiful melody that can be expressed without even knowing the underlying story of rejection. *(And who hasn't experienced that one?)* Don't miss making the most of the climax in the last eight bars! If you want to maximize the benefits of this volume I suggest that you determine the overall emotion of each song by studying the lyrics and listening to Sinatra's renditions for he soaks them with soulful feelings.

Now **Dancing On The Ceiling** is the "mildest" of the songs in this volume but certainly conjures up images of longing for your loved one. I love to play (or sing) the verses of these great songs for they introduce the story so well and in many ways without them there's a bit of incompleteness. While playing the notes of the melody try to permeate them with the emotion of the lyrics. With **Dancing On The Ceiling** we have more of a fantasizing scenario than a "poor me" or victim persona.

This next one says it all in the title! **I'll Never Be The Same!** *Stars have lost their glitter for me. Nothing's what it once used to be.* How final and hopeless! Think of it kind of like Method Acting but don't get sucked into it. When the sad or scary movie is over, you shouldn't hang on to those feelings you've experienced, right? For my ending I decided to lighten it up a bit and quote Stravinsky's Rite of Spring!

The wonderful Rodgers and Hart song **It Never Entered My Mind** is what I would call a tone poem and although the melody is gorgeous, Lorenz Hart's lyrics are nothing short of extraordinary! Coming out of the bridge, he writes: *You have what I lack myself and now I even have to scratch my back myself.* I know what you're thinking, a tall order to translate that into musical tones but it makes the difference between a dry, technically correct performance and one that "moves" the listener!

The next song **Can't We Be Friends** has a lilting beat that belies the pain of a relationship that went "south", in other words, from a romance to the dreaded "friend" label. And here is where the verse is vital by describing the scene. Notice that the background is no longer a lush orchestral one but simply the rhythm section so as to eliminate any distractions and present the unhappy story with no frills. The title message just gets repeated to remind us of the all-pervasive sadness that lurks throughout this song with Frank accentuating the negative at the very end: **Can't We Be *Just* Friends?**

With **I See Your Face Before Me,** all you have to do is play the melody and add a few ornaments and the Impressionistic orchestration will take care of making you sound good. It's rare in a musician's career that he has the opportunity to play with world-class backgrounds like this, so enjoy!

This great Hoagy Carmichael song **I Get Along Without You Very Well** is another tone poem treatment by Riddle that has some challenges in it because in order to fully express the sorrow filled sarcasm in the lyrics, Sinatra apparently felt a need for rubato throughout instead of tempo! The several *"of course I do"* after the title line *I get along without you very well* followed by *except....* sets the pattern of the story which I tried to create instrumentally. Have patience with yourself on this one for it's a bit challenging and requires concentration to get into alignment with the flow of the orchestration. Of course, it should be consoling to remember that when Frank recorded this, Nelson *followed him* while conducting the orchestra!

Ah, how nice to have tempo back to play with! **This Love Of Mine** just flows so nice 'n easy (pun intended). Enjoy the smooth ride on this sweet background and sing, sing, sing! No, not that Sing, Sing, Sing!

And last but certainly not least the great Cole Porter classic **What Is This Thing Called Love** that I and most jazz musicians usually play as a fast tune and even as a Bossa Nova. Now here, perhaps because this is more of a Sinatra saloon song, you know, like One For My Baby And One More For The Road so that at this really slow tempo it becomes a vehicle to express the subtle pathos of the Porter lyric, instrumentally, of course! Here's where the transcribed solo comes in handy for I took more liberty on this and incorporated some of the other steps of my seven step program.

And now some musical trivia for you:

Have you noticed how the length of hit records has changed from three minutes to whatever it takes?

The reason: The 45 rpm and eventually the 33 1/3 rpm Long Playing Record inherited the limitation of the 78 rpm record.

Well, as they say, "That's All Folks." Seriously, may I wish you great success in your ballad playing and as always you may contact me at bobzottola@naplesjazzlovers.com if you have questions or just would like to share your experience using this volume six.

All the best!
Bob Zottola

Music Minus One Trumpet
Also suitable for any B♭ Instrument

6846

THE FINE ART OF
BALLAD PLAYING
Standards for Trumpet, Vol. 6

CONTENTS

SOLO B♭ TRUMPET

In The Wee Small Hours of the Morning

Words by Bob Hilliard
Music by David Mann

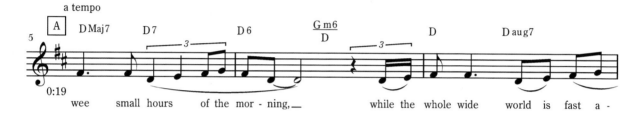

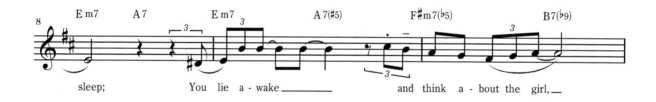

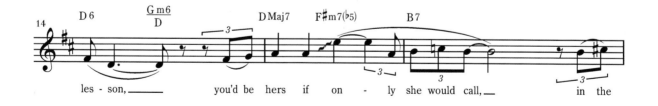

SOLO B♭ TRUMPET

I'll Be Around

Words and Music by Alec Wilder

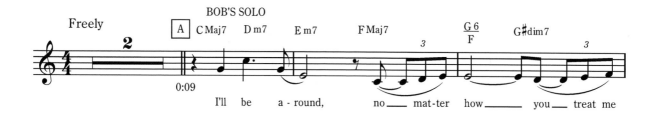

I'll be a-round, no mat-ter how you treat me now.

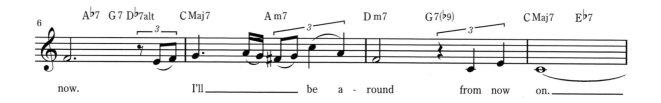

I'll be a-round from now on.

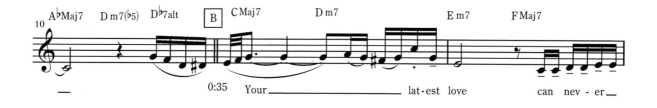

Your lat-est love can nev-er

last and when it's past I'll be a-round when he's

gone. Good-bye a-gain, and if you find a love like

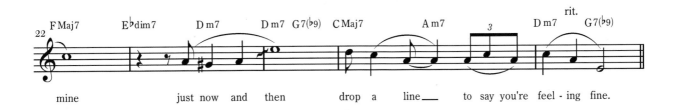

mine — just now and then — drop a line___ to say you're feel-ing fine.

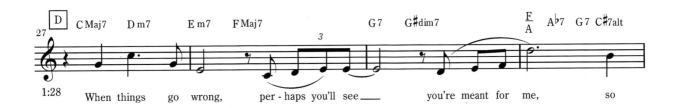

1:28 When things go wrong, per-haps you'll see___ you're meant for me, so

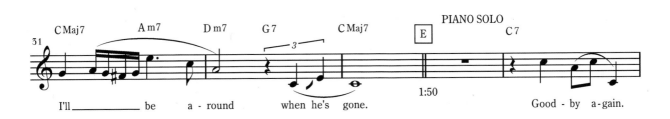

I'll___ be a-round when he's gone. 1:50 Good-by a-gain.

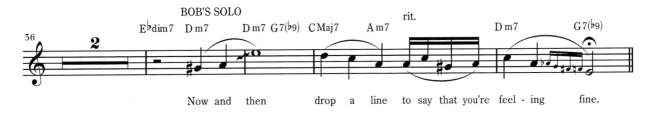

Now and then drop a line to say that you're feel-ing fine.

2:19 And when___ things go wrong, per-haps you'll see you're meant for me so

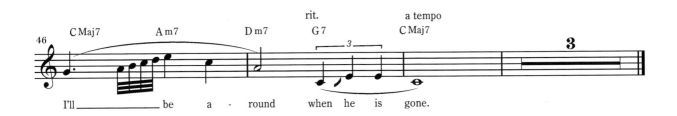

I'll___ be a-round when he is gone.

SOLO B♭ TRUMPET

Dancing On the Ceiling

Words by Lorenz Hart
Music by Richard Rodgers

The world is lyr-i-cal, because a mir-a-cle has brought my lov-er to

me. Though she's some oth er place, her face_____ I

see. At night I creep in bed, and nev er sleep in bed,

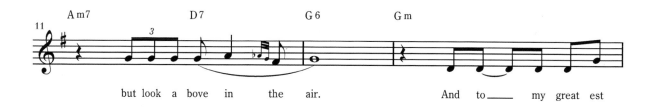

but look a bove in the air. And to_____ my great est

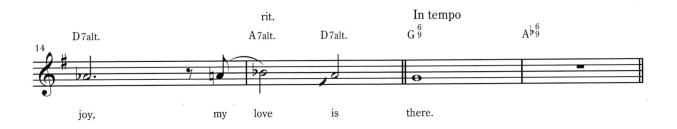

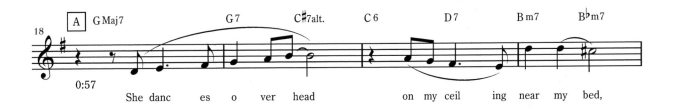

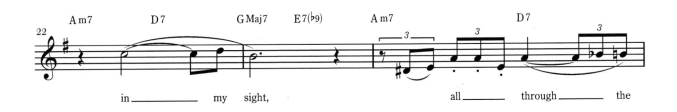

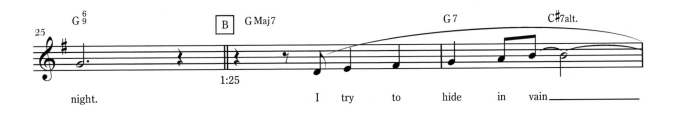

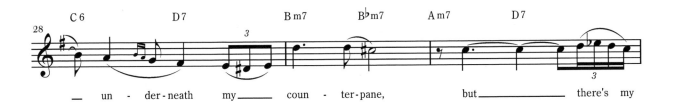

love up_____ there a - bove.

I whis - per "Go away my lov - er, it's not fair."_____

But I'm___ so grate-ful to dis - cov - er that she's still there._____

I love my ceil - ing more__ since it is a

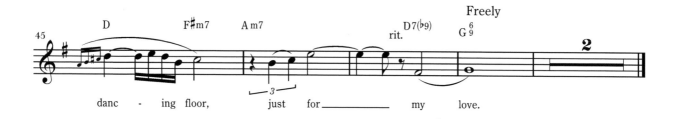

danc - ing floor, just for_____ my love.

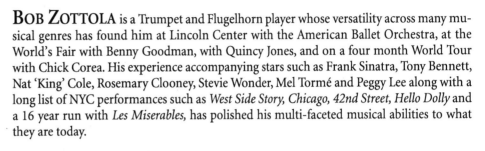

BOB ZOTTOLA is a Trumpet and Flugelhorn player whose versatility across many musical genres has found him at Lincoln Center with the American Ballet Orchestra, at the World's Fair with Benny Goodman, with Quincy Jones, and on a four month World Tour with Chick Corea. His experience accompanying stars such as Frank Sinatra, Tony Bennett, Nat 'King' Cole, Rosemary Clooney, Stevie Wonder, Mel Tormé and Peggy Lee along with a long list of NYC performances such as *West Side Story, Chicago, 42nd Street, Hello Dolly* and a 16 year run with *Les Miserables,* has polished his multi-faceted musical abilities to what they are today.

Brazilian Bossa Novas by Jobim..MMO CD 3871
10 classic Jobim Bossa Novas. Complete note for note transcriptions along with chords and original melody line. May be used by all Bb instruments. *The Girl from Ipanema • So Danco Samba • Once I Loved • Dindi • One Note Samba • Meditation • How Insensitive • Triste • Corcovado • Wave*

Standards for Trumpet, Vol. 1 ....MMO CD 6841
Standards performed with big band, and also smaller ensembles. Complete transcriptions of every note are provided plus melody line, chords and lyrics. The CD contains a complete performance of each piece in digital stereo, followed by a second digital stereo version minus the soloist. *When You're Smiling (The Whole World Smiles with You) • I'm in the Mood for Love • Blue Bossa • How Do You Keep the Music Playing? • It's Only a Paper Moon • Samba de Orfeo • Blue Moon • You Must Believe in Spring • Black Orpheus • Fly Me To the Moon (In Other Words)*

Standards for Trumpet, Vol. 2: *Pure Imagination*...................................MMO CD 6842
These albums are dual purpose. They can be listened to as renditions of some of the finest songs in what has been called The Great American Song Book and in the traditional 'minus one' format as a practice and educational tool. *September in the Rain • Pure Imagination • I May Be Wrong • Here's That Rainy Day • This Happy Madness • Body and Soul • Smoke Gets In Your Eyes • Always • Embraceable You • I Got Rhythm (slow) • I Got Rhythm (original)*

Standards for Trumpet, Vol. 3: *Gold Standards* ....MMO CD 6843
Still more standards from the Great American Song Book, music that should be in every musician's library! *If I Should Lose You • Darn That Dream • Too Marvelous For Words • I Concentrate On You • Teach Me Tonight • Gentle Rain • Three Little Words • That's All • Little White Lies • Have Yourself A Merry Little Christmas*

Standards for Trumpet, Vol. 4: *Stardust*..MMO CD 6844
This 4th album leads off with a song that perhaps personifies our thoughts about this series - The Best Is Yet To Come. *The Best Is Yet To Come • I Had The Craziest Dream • Baubles, Bangles and Beads • Cinema Paradiso • Can't Take My Eyes Off Of You • My Funny Valentine • Brazil • Stardust • Oh, Lady Be Good • The Christmas Song*

Standards for Trumpet, Vol. 5: *Arrangements by Riddle* ....MMO CD 6845
The CD contains a complete performance of each piece in digital stereo, followed by a second digital stereo version minus the soloist. May be used by all Bb instruments. *You Make Me Feel So Young • Fools Rush In • My Baby Just Cares For Me • The More I See You • Everywhere You Go • When Your Lover Has Gone • Day In-Day Out • It's A Sin To Tell A Lie • Near You • You're Driving Me Crazy*

Music Minus One   *The mark of quality in accompaniment editions since 1950*
Tel: **1.800.669.7464** US • **1.914.592.1188** international • **www.musicminusone.com**

SOLO B♭ TRUMPET

I'll Never Be The Same

Words and Music by Gus Kahn,
Matt Malneck and Frank Signorelli

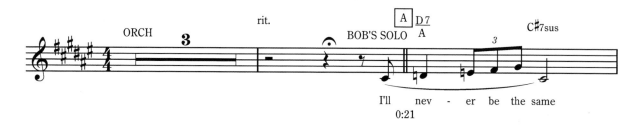

I'll nev - er be the same

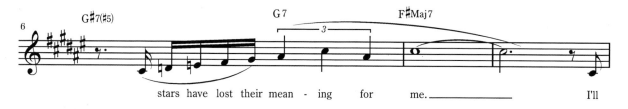

stars have lost their mean - ing for me. I'll

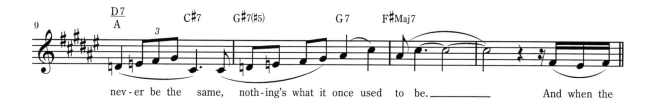

nev - er be the same, noth - ing's what it once used to be. And when the

song - birds that sing tell me it's spring, I can't be - lieve their

song. Once love was king, but kings can be

SOLO B♭ TRUMPET

It Never Entered My Mind

Words by Lorenz Hart
Music by Richard Rodgers

Freely

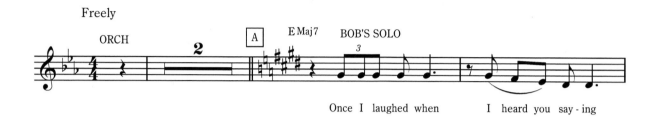

Once I laughed when I heard you say-ing

that__ I'd be play-ing____ sol - i - taire, un - eas - y____ in__ my

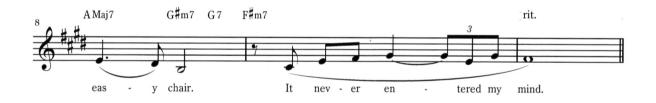

eas - y chair. It nev - er en - tered my mind.

Once you told me I was mis - tak - en, that I'd a - wak - en____

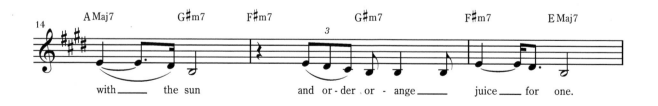

with____ the sun and or - der or - ange____ juice____ for one.

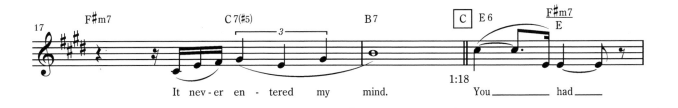

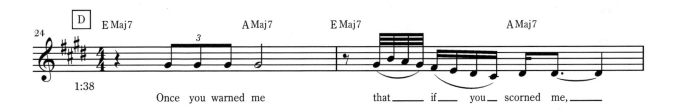

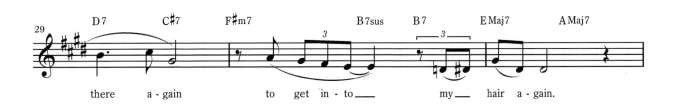

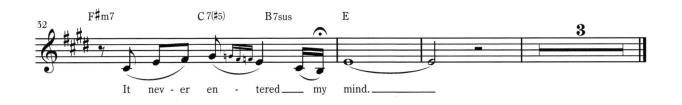

SOLO B♭ TRUMPET

Can't We Be Friends

Words by Paul James
Music by Kay Swift

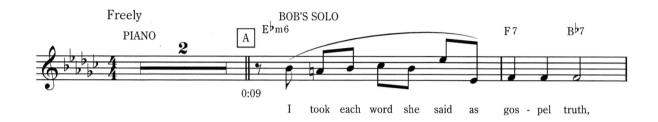

I took each word she said as gos-pel truth,

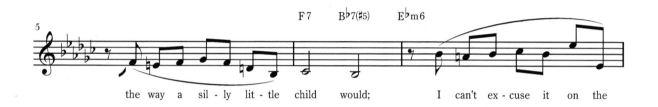

the way a sil-ly lit-tle child would; I can't ex-cuse it on the

grounds of youth, I was no babe in the wild, wild wood.

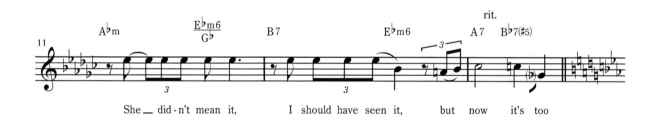

She __ did-n't mean it, I should have seen it, but now it's too

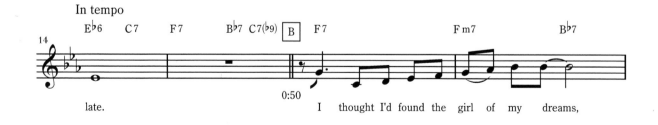

late. I thought I'd found the girl of my dreams,

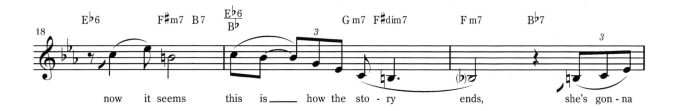

now it seems this is___ how the sto - ry ends, she's gon - na

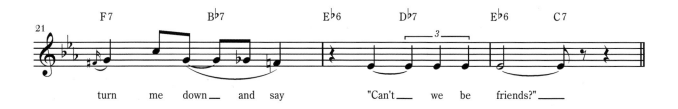

turn me down__ and say "Can't__ we be friends?"__

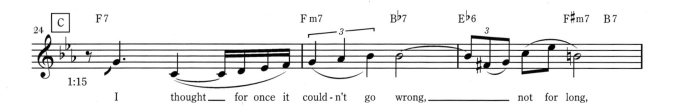

I thought__ for once it could - n't go wrong,_____ not for long,

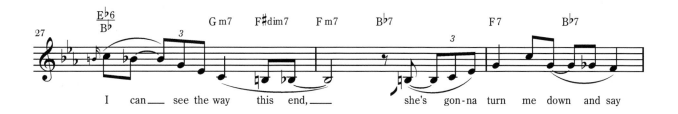

I can__ see the way this end,__ she's gon - na turn me down and say

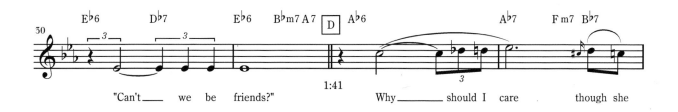

"Can't__ we be friends?" Why_____ should I care though she

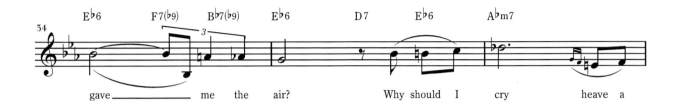

gave _____ me the air? Why should I cry heave a

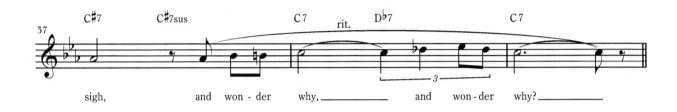

sigh, and won - der why, _____ and won - der why? _____

I _____ thought I'd found the gal I could trust, what a bust,

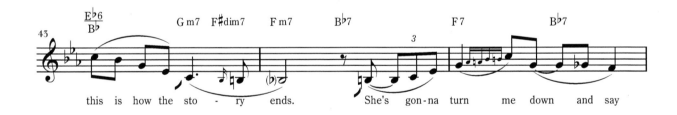

this is how the sto - ry ends. She's gon-na turn me down and say

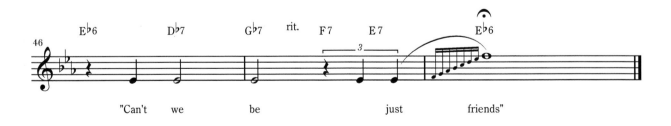

"Can't we be just friends"

Music Minus One
DISTINGUISHED ACCOMPANIMENT EDITIONS

Trumpet in B-flat

Chamber Classics
Baroque Brass and Beyond: Quintets ....MMO CD 3808 $29.98
Classic Pieces for Trumpet & Organ ....MMO CD 3840 $29.98
Classic Trumpet Solos w/Piano ....MMO CD 3830 $29.98
Music for Brass Ensemble ....MMO CD 3805 $29.98
STRAVINSKY L'Histoire du Soldat ....MMO CD 3835 $29.98
Trumpet Artistry: Classical Solos ....MMO CD 3855 $29.98
Trumpet Pieces: Brass Quintets ....MMO CD 3827 $29.98

Folk, Bluegrass and Country
Boots Randolph, vol. 2: Embraceable Tunes ....MMO CD 4276 $24.98
Boots Randolph: Nashville Classics..........................MMO CD 4223 $24.98
Boots Randolph: Some Favorite Songs
  Standards with Band...MMO CD 4275 $24.98

Inspirational Classics
Boots Randolph: When the Spirit Moves You ....MMO CD 4222 $24.98
Brass Trax: David O'Neill.......................................MMO CD 3833 $24.98
Christmas Memories ....MMO CDG 1203 $19.98
Touch the Spirit (Wayne Naus) ....MMO CD 6839 $24.98
Trumpet Triumphant: David O'Neill ....MMO CD 3834 $24.98

Instrumental Classics with Orchestra
Art of the Solo Trumpet w/Orch ....MMO CD 3807 $29.98
ARUTIUNIAN Conc.; GOEDICKE Etude.......................MMO CD 3846 $39.98
Band Aids: Concert Band Favorites.........................MMO CD 3832 $29.98
Classics for Trumpet and Concert Band ....MMO CD 3849 $29.98
Encore! Another Night at the Opera:
  Opera Arias Trumpet & Orch, v. II........................MMO CD 3848 $24.98
First Chair Trumpet Solos w/Orch ....MMO CD 3806 $29.98
Concerti HAYDN Eb, HobVIIe:1;
  TELEMANN D, TWV53:D2; FASCH D.....................MMO CD 3801 $39.98
A Night at the Opera:
  Opera Arias for Trumpet and Orch, v. I.................MMO CD 3847 $24.98
Popular Concert Favorites Trumpet ....MMO CD 3831 $24.98
SOUSA Marches plus BEETHOVEN,
  BERLIOZ, STRAUSS..MMO CD 3810 $29.98
VIVALDI Conc. for Two Trumpets.............................MMO CD 3842 $39.98

Jazz, Standards and Big Band
2+2=5: A Study Odd Times ....MMO CD 2043 $19.98
Bacharach Revisited ....MMO CD 3854 $24.98
Back to Basie, Back to Basics (Peter Ecklund) ....MMO CD 3862 $19.98
Bluesaxe: Blues for Sax ....MMO CD 4205 $19.98
Days of Wine & Roses ....MMO CD 4210 $19.98
For Saxes Only: Bob Wilber ....MMO CD 4204 $19.98
From Dixie to Swing ....MMO CD 3826 $19.98
The Further Adventure of Bix Beiderbecke ....MMO CD 3853 $19.98
Isle of Orleans..MMO CD 3850 $19.98
New Orleans Classics ....MMO CD 3851 $19.98
Northern Lights ....MMO CD 2003 $19.98
PCH Pacific Coast Horns, vol. 1: Bugler's Holiday ....MMO CD 6828 $19.98

PCH Pacific Coast Horns, vol. 2:
  Fascinatin' Rhythm (Int-Adv) ....MMO CD 6829 $19.98
PCH Pacific Coast Horns, vol. 3:
  Modern Trumpet Solos ....MMO CD 6830 $19.98
Play Ballads w/a Band ....MMO CD 3841 $19.98
Play Lead in a Sax Section: Bob Wilber All-Stars.....MMO CD 4209 $19.98
Jazz Flute Jam ....MMO CD 3376 $19.98
Standards for Trumpet, vol. 1 (Bob Zottola)............MMO CD 6841 $24.98
Standards for Trumpet, vol. 2:
  Pure Imagination (Bob Zottola) ....MMO CD 6842 $24.98
Standards for Trumpet, vol. 3 (Bob Zottola)............MMO CD 6843 $24.98
Standards for Trumpet, vol. 4:
  Stardust (Bob Zottola) ....MMO CD 6844 $24.98
Standards for Trumpet, vol. 5 (Bob Zottola)............MMO CD 6845 $24.98
Standards for Trumpet, vol. 6:
  In the Wee Small Hours (Bob Zottola) ....MMO CD 6846 $24.98
Studio City ....MMO CD 2023 $19.98
Swing with a Band ....MMO CD 3843 $19.98
Take One (minus Lead Trumpet) ....MMO CD 2013 $19.98
The Swing Era: Munich Brass ....MMO CD 3856 $19.98
Chicago-Style Jam Session ....MMO CD 3844 $19.98
Adventures in N.Y. & Chicago Jazz ....MMO CD 3845 $19.98
Trumpet Duets in Jazz - 18 Duets (Burt Collins) ......MMO CD 3859 $19.98
20 Dixieland Classics ....MMO CD 3824 $19.98
20 Rhythm Bkgrds to Standards ....MMO CD 3825 $19.98
When Jazz Was Young ....MMO CD 3829 $19.98

Latin Classics
JOBIM Brazilian Bossa Novas w/Strings.................MMO CD 3871 $24.98

Laureate Master Series Concert Solos
Beginning Contest Solos, v. I (Schwarz) ....MMO CD 3811 $19.98
Beginning Contest Solos, v. II (Ghitalla)..................MMO CD 3812 $19.98
Int. Solos, v. I (Nagel) ....MMO CD 3813 $19.98
Int. Solos, v. II (Schwarz) ....MMO CD 3814 $19.98
Int. Solos, v. III (Schwarz) ....MMO CD 3817 $19.98
Int. Solos, v. IV (Ghitalla) ....MMO CD 3816 $19.98
Int. Solos, v. V (Crisara) ....MMO CD 3822 $19.98
Advanced Solos, v. I (Nagel) ....MMO CD 3815 $19.98
Advanced Solos, v. II (Nagel) ....MMO CD 3818 $19.98
Advanced Solos, v. III (Ghitalla).............................MMO CD 3819 $19.98

Student Series
Arban Duets ....MMO CD 3809 $24.98
Classic Themes: 27 Easy Songs ....MMO CD 3837 $19.98
Easy Jazz Duets 2 Trumpets/Rhythm Section ....MMO CD 3804 $19.98
Take a Chorus ....MMO CD 7008 $19.98
Teacher's Partner: Basic Studies ....MMO CD 3823 $19.98
Trumpet Solos: Student Level, v. I.........................MMO CD 3802 $19.98
Trumpet Solos: Student Level, v. II ....MMO CD 3803 $19.98
Twelve Classic Jazz Standards ....MMO CD 7010 $19.98
Twelve More Classic Jazz Standards ....MMO CD 7011 $19.98
World Favorites: 41 Easy Selections......................MMO CD 3836 $19.98

All Prices Subject To Change

SOLO B♭ TRUMPET

I See Your Face Before Me

Words by Howard Dietz
Music by Arthur Schwartz

MMO 6846

SOLO B♭ TRUMPET

I Get Along Without You Very Well
(Except Sometimes)

Words and Music by
Hoagy Carmichael

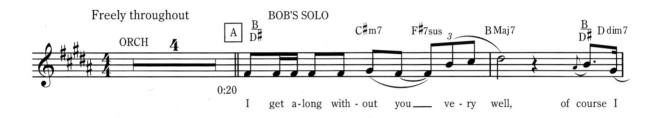

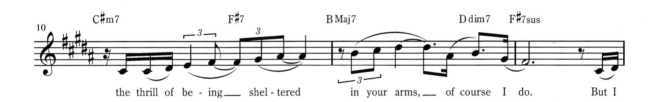

Inspired by a poem written by J.B. Thompson
Copyright © 1938, 1939 by Songs Of Peer, Ltd.
Copyrights Renewed
This arrangement Copyright © 2012 by Songs Of Peer, Ltd.
International Copyright Secured   All Rights Reserved
Reprinted by permission of Hal Leonard Corporation

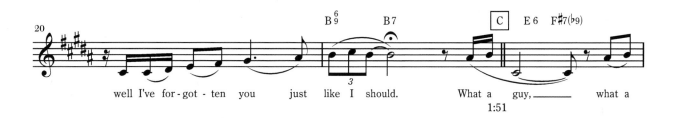

well I've for-got-ten you just like I should. What a guy,_____ what a

1:51

fool_____ am I_____ to think_____ my break-ing heart could kid the moon. What's in

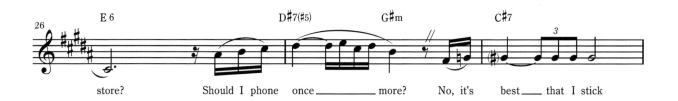

store? Should I phone once_____ more? No, it's best_____ that I stick

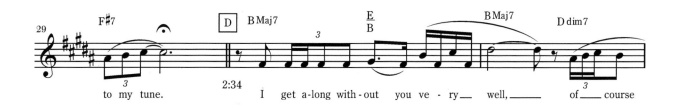

to my tune. I get a-long with-out you ve-ry_____ well,_____ of_____ course

2:34

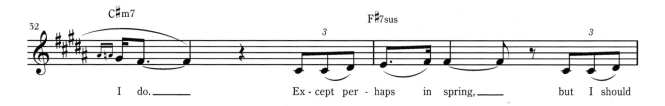

I do._____ Ex-cept per-haps in spring,_____ but I should

ne-ver think of spring, for that would sure-ly break my heart in two._____

SOLO B♭ TRUMPET

This Love Of Mine

Words and Music by Sol Parker,
Henry W. Sanicola and Frank Sinatra

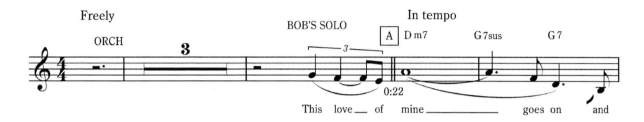

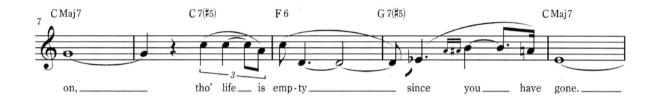

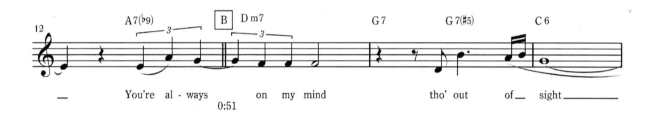

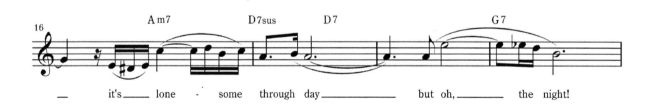

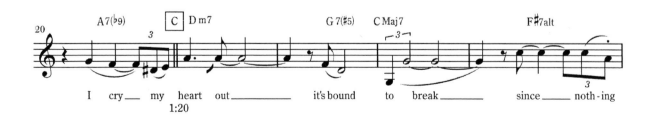

SOLO B♭ TRUMPET

What Is This Thing Called Love?

Words and Music by COLE PORTER

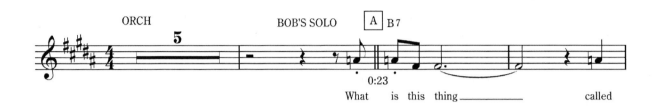

What   is   this   thing____   called

love,____   this   fun - ny   thing____   called

love?____   Just____   who   can   solve____

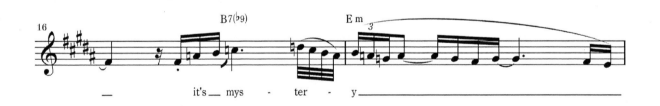

____   it's____ mys - ter - y____

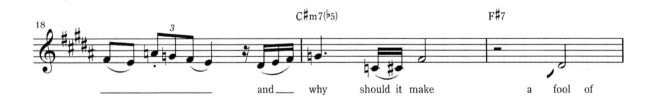

____   and____ why   should   it   make   a   fool   of

me._____

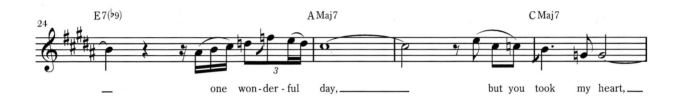

_ one won-der-ful day,_____ but you took my heart,_

_ and you threw my_____ heart a - way._____

That's why I ask_____ the_ Lord up in hea - ven a -

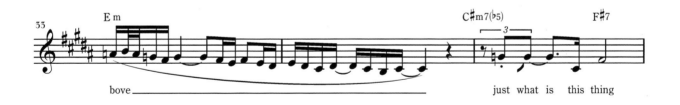

bove_____ just what is this thing

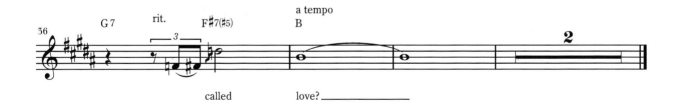

called love?_____

MUSIC MINUS ONE
50 Executive Boulevard
Elmsford, New York 10523-1325
800-669-7464 (US) • 914-592-1188 (International)

www.musicminusone.com
e-mail: info@musicminusone.com

MMO 6846

ISBN 1-59615-839-9